piano | vocal | guitar

nichole nordeman
this mystery

ISBN 0-634-02035-8

HAL•LEONARD® CORPORATION
7777 W. BLUEMOUND RD. P.O. BOX 13819 MILWAUKEE, WI 53213

Visit Hal Leonard Online at
www.halleonard.com

contents

THIS MYSTERY

Words and Music by
NICHOLE NORDEMAN

TREMBLE

Words and Music by
NICHOLE NORDEMAN

Moderately

Ah da da da ____ da da ____ da da da da. ____

Have ____ I ____ come too ca - sual - ly, ____ be - cause it seems to me ____

to think that I'd ap - pear ____ e - ven slight - ly cav - a -

Na da da _____ na. ____

FOOL FOR YOU

Words and Music by
NICHOLE NORDEMAN

Moderately bright

There are times _ when faith and com-mon sense _ do not _ a - lign,
I ad - mit _ that in my dark-est hours _ I've asked, _ "What if?" _

when hard - core ev - i - dence _ of You _ is hard _ to _ find. _
What if _ we cre - a - ted _ some kind _ of man - made faith like this? _

HELP ME BELIEVE

Words and Music by
NICHOLE NORDEMAN

SMALL ENOUGH

Words and Music by
NICHOLE NORDEMAN

Slowly and tenderly

Oh, _____ great _____ God, be small e-nough to hear _____ me now.

There were times when __ I was cry-ing from the dark of Dan-iel's den, _ and I have asked __ You once or twice_ if You would part_ the sea _ a-gain. _ But to-

LOOKIN' AT YOU
(Lookin' At Me)

Words and Music by NICHOLE NORDEMAN,
MARK HAMMOND and JILL TOMALTY

Moderate beat

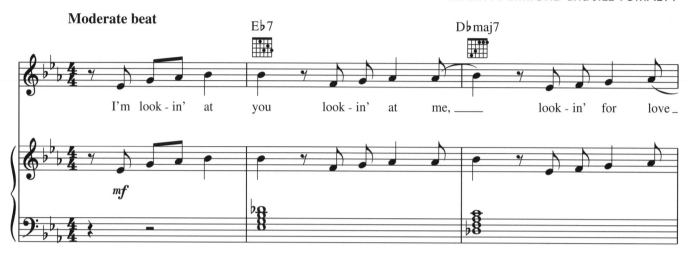

I'm look-in' at you look-in' at me, _____ look-in' for love _____

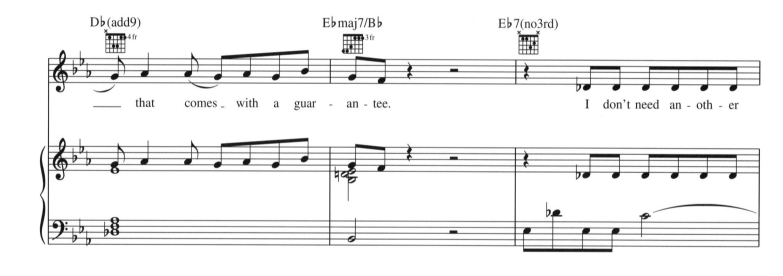

_____ that comes _ with a guar - an - tee. I don't need an - oth - er

friend tryin' to tell me some-thin'. I don't need some-bod - y's ex - pert ad - vice. _____

AS

Words and Music by
STEVIE WONDER

Original key: Db major. This edition has been transposed down one half-step to be more playable.

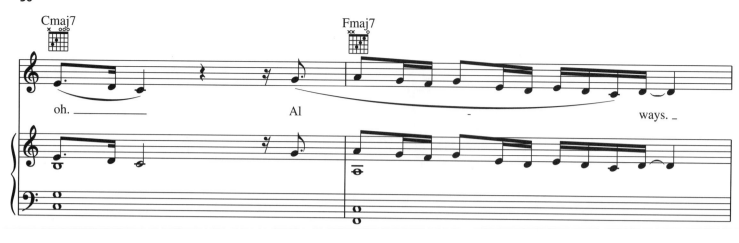

oh. _____ Al - ways. _

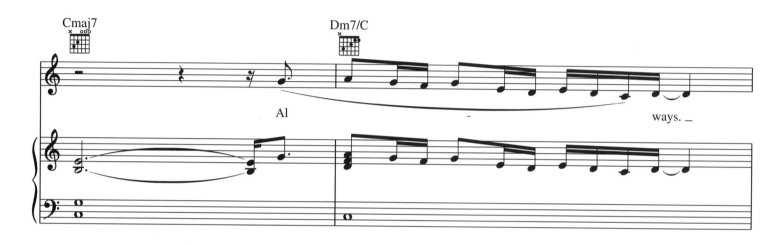

Al - ways. _

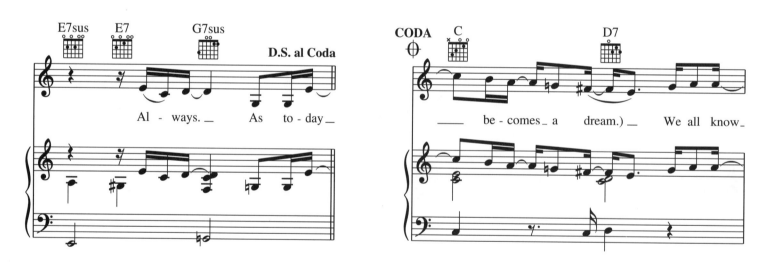

Al - ways. _ As to-day _

CODA

_____ be - comes _ a dream.) _ We all know _

_____ some - times _ life's hates and trou - bles _____ can make _ you wish _

HOME

Words and Music by NICHOLE NORDEMAN
and MARK HAMMOND

PLEASE COME

Words and Music by
NICHOLE NORDEMAN

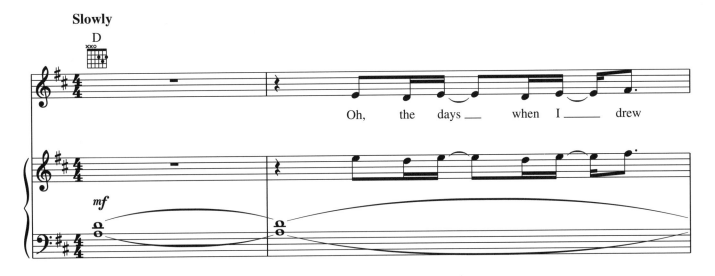

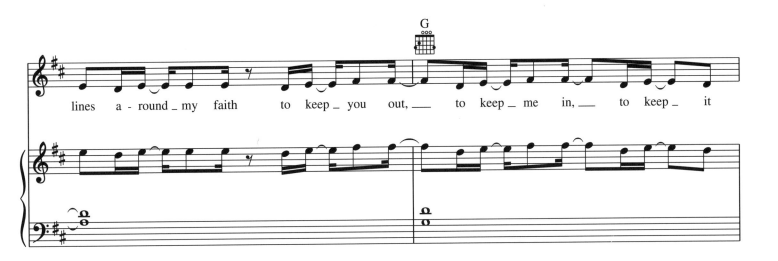

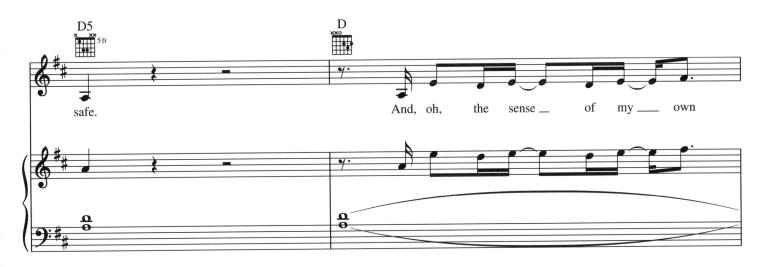

Original key: Db major. This edition has been transposed up one half-step to be more playable.

EVERY SEASON

Words and Music by
NICHOLE NORDEMAN

Moderately flowing

thanks for what has been and what's to come. You

are au - tumn.

WHY

Words and Music by
NICHOLE NORDEMAN

RIVER GOD

Words and Music by
NICHOLE NORDEMAN

Moderately, with freedom

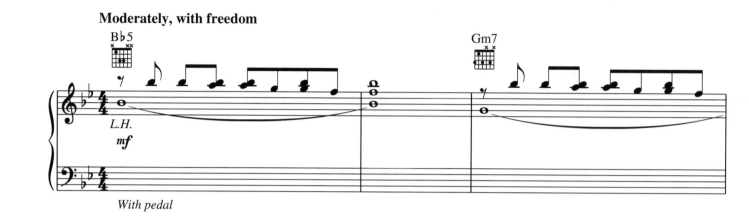

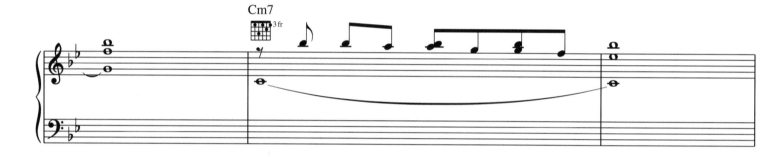

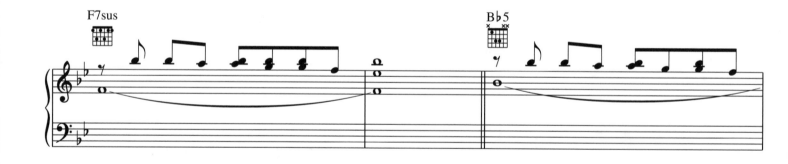

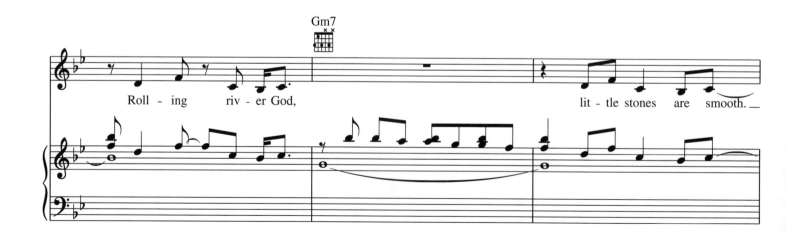

Roll - ing riv - er God,   lit - tle stones are smooth. __

TO KNOW YOU

Words and Music by NICHOLE NORDEMAN
and MARK HAMMOND

Moderately slow

It's well __ past mid-night and I'm a-wake __ with ques-tions that won't wait __ for day-light, sep-a-rat-ing fact __ from my i-mag--i-nar--y fic-tion on this shelf of my __ con-vic-tion. I

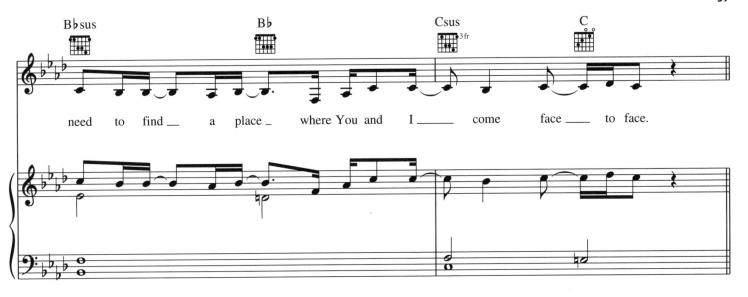

need to find ___ a place ___ where You and I ___ come face ___ to face.

Thom - as need - ed proof that You ___ had real - ly ris - en
Nic - o - de - mus could not un - der - stand ___ how You could

un - de - feat - ed. When he placed ___ his fin - gers where the
tru - ly free ___ us. He strug - gled with ___ the im - age of a

nails once broke Your skin, __ did his faith fi - n'lly be - gin? ____ I've
grown man born a - gain. __ We might have been good friends, __ cuz

lied if I've __ de - nied __ the com-mon ground __ I've shared __ with him. ___ And I, __
some-times I ___ still ques - tion, too, how ea - si - ly we come to You. __ But I, __

I real - ly want __ to know __ You.   I

You. Ah.

Ah.

WHO YOU ARE

Words and Music by NICHOLE NORDEMAN
and MARK HAMMOND

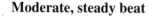

cer - tain that __ I knew __ You at the ten - der age __ of twelve. You'd so

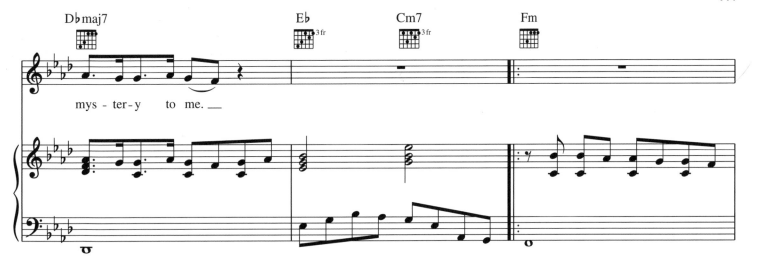

mys - ter-y   to me. __

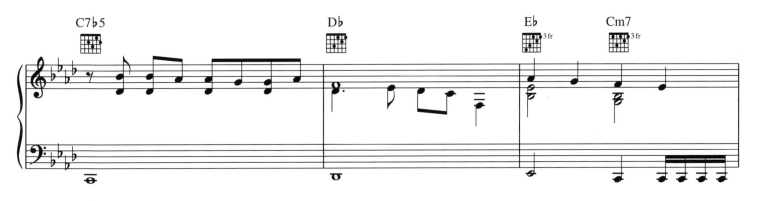

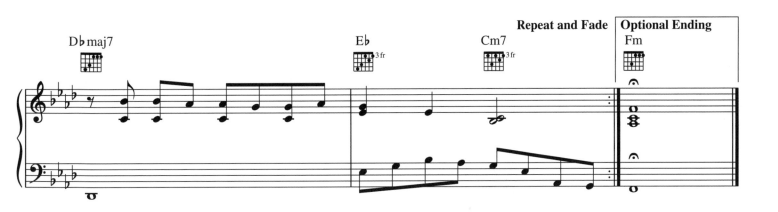

CONTEMPORARY CHRISTIAN FOLIOS

available from Hal Leonard

SUSAN ASHTON – SO FAR ...
THE BEST OF SUSAN ASHTON

12 songs, featuring her #1 hits. Songs include: Stand • Hide Or Seek • Here In My Heart • Grand Canyon • and more.

00306061 Piano / Vocal / Guitar $12.95

SUSAN ASHTON

Matching folio featuring: Agree To Disagree • Hold The Intangible • Remember Not • A Rose Is A Rose • Waiting For Your Love To Come Down • and more. Arranged for keyboard and medium voice with chord symbols.

00306099 Piano / Vocal / Guitar................................$10.95

MICHAEL CARD –
JOY IN THE JOURNEY

Matching folio to his compilation of 10 years of hits. 18 songs, including: El Shaddai • The Final Word • Known By Scars • and more.

00306152 Piano / Vocal / Guitar $12.95

STEVEN CURTIS CHAPMAN –
HEAVEN IN THE REAL WORLD

Matching folio with 12 songs, including: Heaven In The Real World • King Of The Jungle • The Mountain • Love And Learn • and more.

00306151 Piano / Vocal / Guitar $14.95

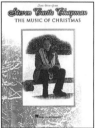

STEVEN CURTIS CHAPMAN –
THE MUSIC OF CHRISTMAS

12 traditional favorites, including: Angels We Have Heard On High • Carol Of The Bells • Interlude: The Music Of Christmas • Our God Is With Us • Precious Promise • This Baby • and more.

00313031 Piano / Vocal / Guitar $14.95

STEVEN CURTIS CHAPMAN –
SIGNS OF LIFE

Matching folio to the newest release from this best-selling, award-winning artist. 12 songs, including: Celebrate You • Free • Lord Of The Dance • What Would I Say • Signs Of Life • and more.

00306119 Piano / Vocal / Guitar $14.95

STEVEN CURTIS CHAPMAN –
TWENTY FAVORITES

This folio, complete with photos, features 20 songs from his entire career, including: Don't Let The Fire Die • For The Sake Of The Call • Go There With You • The Great Adventure • I Will Be Here • More To This Life • My Turn Now • When You Are A Soldier • and more.

00306150 Piano / Vocal / Guitar $14.95

DELIRIOUS – SONGS FROM CUTTING
EDGE

15 songs, including: All I Want Is You • Did You Feel the Mountain Tremble? • I Could Sing of Your Love Forever • I'm Not Ashamed • I've Found Jesus • Lord, You Have My Heart • and more.

00306243 Piano / Vocal / Guitar $17.95

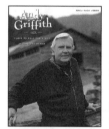

STEVE GREEN – THE FIRST NOEL

Matching folio to Steve Green's newest Christmas recording. Songs include: Midnight Clear • Jesu, Light Of Lights • What Child Is This? • Rose Of Bethlehem • and six others.

00306115 Piano / Vocal / Guitar $14.95

ANDY GRIFFITH –
I LOVE TO TELL THE STORY

Souvenir matching folio to the popular recording. Contains photos and background information on Andy plus notes on the hymns. 23 songs, including: How Great Thou Art • The Old Rugged Cross • Sweet Hour Of Prayer • Wayfaring Stranger • What A Friend We Have In Jesus • and more.

00306116 Piano / Vocal / Guitar $14.95

CHERI KEAGGY – MY FAITH WILL STAY

Matching folio with 10 songs, including: Beautiful Little Girl • He Will Look After You • Heavenly Father • In Remembrance Of Me • Keep On Shinin' • Lay It Down • The Love Of God • My Faith Will Stay • Sweet Peace Of God • We All Need Jesus.

00306107 Piano / Vocal / Guitar $16.95

GIVING YOU THE REST OF MY LIFE

13 contemporary Christian classics from Steven Curtis Chapman, Susan Ashton, Steve Green, Michael English, and more. Songs include: All I Ever Wanted • Friends For Life • Go There With You • Over And Over • Wedding Song (There Is Love) • and more.

00313068 Piano / Vocal / Guitar $10.95

FOR MORE INFORMATION, SEE YOUR LOCAL MUSIC DEALER,
OR WRITE TO:

HAL•LEONARD®
CORPORATION

7777 W. BLUEMOUND RD. P.O. BOX 13819 MILWAUKEE, WI 53213

0199